Adopting
Courage:

A survivor's guide
to triumph after trauma

Written By:

Michelle Dennis

Copyright ©2019 Michelle Dennis

Published by Live Limitless
Authors Academy & Publishing Co.
Publishing@sierrarainge.com

Michelle Dennis Contact Information :
Email: michelledennis.md@gmail.com
Website: www.enuffisenuff.guru

Printed in the United States of America
Cover Design by: Adam I. Wade
Cover Photo by: Joyanne Panton Photography

Library of Congress Number: 2019915411

Dedication

This book is dedicated to my Son J'veon, who inspires me daily to be the best version of myself, to my daughter Jacquline who compels me to live without limits, my granddaughter Ella who lights up my world, and my love Timothy Mosley who has taught me the transformative power of loving hard.

Adopting Courage

Acknowledgements

I want to thank God for His amazing grace. To my children who shower me with unconditional love, my life is filled with purpose each day because of you. Thank you for loving me beyond my imperfections, I appreciate your tender love and patience as I worked to navigate through my Journey. To my brother Aaron and his twin brother Henry, Thank you for being strong and for making a way no matter what obstacles you faced. To my crazy, cool, & honest dad, Vernon Dennis, for waking us up in the morning blasting Tracy Chapman's, "Fast Car" or "Talkin' about revolution" on repeat. I didn't understand what the songs meant back then but I do now. Thanks dad for being the most annoying, playful, smart, and motivated man that I know. I am forever grateful, eternally thankful and blessed that you loved us all the same. I'd like to express sincere and loving gratitude to Timothy Mosley for all your love and support during this process. I would like to express my gratitude to all the people that were with me on my journey. Vicki Peoples, Tiffani Peoples, Gregory Peoples and Corey Harvey, who were all a huge blessing in my life. When I had no 'one to turn to, they all came together to help me. When I was lost and trying to find a better way for myself, thank you for repeatedly coming to my rescue. I know I bumped my head a lot along the way lol, but you understood me even when I didn't understand myself. In the midst of my bad decisions, you still showed me love and you extended that same love to my children. To my adopted sister Chamica, thank you for so graciously sharing your mother with my brothers and I, you are well appreciated.

To my mom Pat, thank you for your willingness to take my brothers and I in, provide a home for us to grow together in, and most of all for keeping us together. Thank you for all the lessons you've taught me over the years, even the tough love and hard lessons contributed to my growth.

Each of you have played a vital role in my healing, my growth and my evolution. I am better, wiser and stronger because of each of you, your love, your support and your contribution to my evolution of becoming the best version of myself.

I'd like to give a special thanks to Erika Driskell who is the director of Communications for Enuff is Enuff Guru. To Zayd Portillo for his amazing web design and illustrations. Jason Pezant for his creative contribution as an illustrator and artist and Adam Wade for capturing my vision for the book cover and creating a masterpiece that I'm so proud of. To Sierra Rainge my publisher turned friend, I'm so grateful for you and your gift.

Adopting Courage

Table of Contents

Open Letter

I wrote this book because I think it's important that women share their stories. When we are open to talk about the things that we've survived, it gives those who are facing similar storms encouragement to not give up. Read but resist judgement, comparison and pity. We all go through different struggles and are faced with different levels of pain and opposition. My hope is that this book encourages you to face yours plus do the necessary work to heal. Everyone has an opinion but this is my truth.

Adopting Courage

Introduction

"It takes courage to grow up
and become who you really are."
— *E.E. Cummings*

We are all in a state of constant development. Those who choose to heal, to grow, to develop and to evolve, often find themselves in a continued cycle of learning and releasing. As you transform into the highest version of yourself, you will discover that you will be required to release the outdated version of who you used to be at every point of elevation. It is true when they say that elevation requires separation. In fact, I've found it to be the most painful part of the process. In order to operate at your best capacity, you will need to separate from things that drain you, heal from things that have hurt you and offer forgiveness for things that have scorned you. It's simply impossible to grow and stay the same; but It's critical that you release all the mess in your life so that you can become your best.

Experiencing real healing is no overnight process. In fact, with full transparency; as I write this book and share my heart, I find that I am still in a state of healing. Offering encouragement for those who resonate with my story gives me hope that they can learn from the lessons that I've lived through. Making an impact in the lives of those who suffer in silence, those who are victims with no voice and those who are vulnerable to abuse is my motivation for writing. Coming to terms with my own childhood trauma has been a sacred part of my healing process. As you peel back the pages, I want you to be reminded that the journey to healing is a marathon and not a sprint. You can be a masterpiece and a work in progress at the same time. You can heal from childhood trauma, forgive yourself for bad decisions, forgive others for their contribution to your pain and build a life that reflects your wildest dreams.

You don't have to remain confined to the constraints of the chaos you've experienced in your life. You do not have to remain a prisoner of the past afflictions that you have experienced. Like me, you're reading this book because you or someone you know has fallen victim to some sort of abuse, addiction, trauma or other toxic situations that have had a negative impact on their lives, relationships, or both emotional and mental fortitude. What I want you to know is that while what you have suffered through may not have been your fault, your healing is 100 percent your responsibility. You must take ownership of your wellness by making a choice to work on your healing.

I wrote this book to encourage you to gain power over your pain. You deserve to live a life without emotional suffering. When you neglect healing, you give chaos permission to run rampant in your life.

Many times, those who have experienced traumatic experiences tend to block it all out. They refuse to talk about it, they push it to the back of their memories and they cover it will material things, toxic relationships, bad habits or self-sabotaging traits. True healing is having the courage to face your demons. The truth of the matter is, you will never conquer what you are unwilling to confront. Ignoring your pain is a coping mechanism that is only effective short term. It's like gathering all of your trash and then tucking it away in a trashcan, but then neglecting to actually take the trash outside so that it can be properly disposed of. The trash that is bagged and stored, but not dumped, will eventually stink up your home. Much like the baggage we carry in our hearts and minds, the heavy luggage that we refuse to deal with will eventually stink up our lives.

Carrying the weight of brokenness is such a burden to bare. Give yourself a fighting chance to experience love, life, and passion without the negative overshadowing and constant life disruption that unchecked and unhealed trauma can bring.

I know how scary and even overwhelming it can be to peel back the Band-Aid and other surface level barriers we implement to mask our pain, but it's so necessary. Covering up things that you should be casting out only keeps you stuck in undesirable situations that do not reflect God's promise over your life.

What I know for sure is that although you may have emotional scars that work to remind you of hurtful experiences, you can choose today to let it all go. You can choose to change the way you see your situation, you can choose to adopt healthy behaviors and implement lifestyle changes that promote overall wellness. Although you have experienced hard things, you can recover; you just have to be willing to do the inner work to experience transformation.

My experience of being abandoned by my birth mother, and then being enlisted in the state foster system with my siblings has caused catastrophic trauma for my siblings and I. Enduring verbal and sexual abuse from those who were entrusted to care for and protect me tarnished my perception of love. Transitioning from foster care where I was abused sexually and into adoption where I was abused and antagonized mentally and emotionally, completely altered my perspective on what healthy relationships and boundaries should look like. As an adult, I noticed how some of the same dynamics I endured as a child, showed up in my adult life. It showed up in my relationships in terms of my tolerance for dysfunction and mistreatment. It showed up in my lifestyle choices and it showed up in my parenting style. The pain we put off doesn't go away. It just shows up in another area of our lives.

I know that you desire authentic love, peace, happiness and joy. It is God's plan for us all to enjoy and delight in the fruits of the spirit. Not only are you deserving of each of these virtues, but you are also capable. I want to encourage you to embark on this journey to wholeness with me. Through transparent dialogue, I will share my personal stories of trauma and triumph. You will receive interactive coaching and healing techniques from licensed mental health professionals and you will gain insight on effective coping mechanisms, red flags, resources and daily devotion that will aide in your healing process. Although this book has not been designed to be the framework or sole source of clinical insight, it is a valuable supplement that you can incorporate in your treatment.

Transformation is about experiencing different results. When you make a conscious and deliberate effort to work on the things that keep you stuck, you exemplify courage and strength.

Today you may be consumed with fear, brokenness, sadness, depression and thoughts of inadequacy, but by the end of this book, it is my hope that you will have gained the transformative power of ***adopting courage***. That you will be bold enough to release fear and take back your personal power. What I know for sure, is that your best life is on the other side of the things you choose to confront and heal from.

There is life left after loss, there is purpose even after pain and there are certainly moments where you can triumph after trauma.

I want to encourage you to take this journey with me, choose today to release ownership over the things that keep you **oppressed** so that you can adopt hope, healing, wellness, wholeness and ***courage***.

Chapter 1

The *Courage* to Heal

"God Grant me the serenity to accept
the things that I cannot change, the
Courage to change the things that I
can, and the wisdom to know the
difference between the two"

~Serenity prayer

The biggest pitfall that individuals get trapped in after trauma, is the idea and misconception that the things you've been through must define you. There was a point in my life, that if you asked me who I was, or if prompted to describe myself, the first thing that would come to mind was that I was abandoned by my mother, I was a ward of the state and eventually a girl who was adopted. I always saw myself through the lens of my circumstances. When the vision you have for your life is limited to what you've been through, you lose sight of who and what you can be.

I carried the burden of my upbringing with me for years. You would think my attachment to it was a merit, or some sort of badge of honor the way I held on so tightly to it. In actuality it was more like a chip on my shoulder, a void in my heart and a heavy burden I carried dogmatically. It wasn't until I hit the lowest point in my adult life that I opted for therapy. At that point, I had tried everything else and nothing seemed to work. After a few failed attempts to fix things on my own, I chose to finally get help. Working through my childhood emotional injury, I realized that the weight of the pain that I was carrying was a choice. At any point in my life, I could've put it all down. I could have let it all go, I could have learned new ways of living and even unlearned a lot of self-sabotaging habits that were keeping me confined to who I used to be. I had come to a place in my life that who I wanted to be, was more important that who I had always been. I was desperate for change, and so hungry for healing. I was at a place in my life when staying the same hurt way more than the fear of letting go.

It took so much courage to first admit that I was my own worst enemy. I find it to be a little comical now, but the truth of the matter is, I was the "thing that was formed against me that was not allowing myself to prosper". Holding on to the pain and refusing to deal with it was holding me up from healing and subsequently sabotaging my opportunities to experience wholeness and true-life fulfillment. I had to get out of my own way. I had to stop making excuses for my behavior, I had to examine my relationships and then make a conscious decision to love myself better by only engaging in relationships that inspired me, were reciprocal and were healthy for me. I had to gain the *courage* to release the attachments that kept me anchored in the outdated version of myself, the connections that reminded me of my pain, reaffirmed my brokenness and were blocking me from my destiny.

11

Perhaps you've experienced some things in your life that have severely altered your identity. Perhaps you have lost sight of who you are because you are so consumed with the pain that you feel. Maybe you are still angry at the person who has hurt you, or you desire closure by way of an apology. Maybe you don't know how to let go, but you recognize that you need to; You keep running into the same toxic pitfalls in every relationship; every good thing in your life tends to flee, and you keep finding yourself in new situations that are governed by the same story.

If you desire something different in your life, you must realize that it is truly impossible to experience a different result with the same behavior. In fact, Albert Einstein would deem you a bit insane to expect anything new from old ways of doing things.

I know all too well, the frustration of living through the same old thing and reliving the same old pain. The good news, is that you don't have to stay where you are. No matter how low you feel, how much it hurts, how much it broke your heart or how much it changed your life; you are more powerful than you can ever imagine. You have an incredible grace to get through the hardest of things; and not only can you get through it, but you can heal from it.

So many of us find that we have the strength to will our way through the toughest of times. The problem is that once we get through it, we continue to hang on to it. We allow our minds to replay it, we talk about it any chance we get, we use it as an excuse for bad behavior and poor choices, and we allow it to govern our lives. It becomes a place of comfort, but nothing ever grows in a comfort zone.

It's always easier to stay the same, I mean think about it, in order to stay the same, you literally don't have to do anything. The truth of the matter is, comfort zones don't keep our lives safe, they keep our lives small. Your comfort zone only confines you to what you've already been through while causing you to sacrifice the beauty of new beginnings.

You can decide today that you will honor the possibilities of a happier, joy filled healthy life by letting go of the things that are holding you back.

The trauma you have experienced is not your whole story, it's only a chapter in your book. At any time you can turn the page and even write a whole new chapter. You can begin again, you can start over a million times if you need to. Give yourself permission to get up, to try again, to choose healing, to choose happiness, to choose growth, to choose to do a new thing.

I get so excited thinking about God's amazing grace and how He gives us the power to turn our trauma into triumph.

You have lived through difficult moments, and the profound thing about it is that you can keep on living.

You survived things that would have destroyed others, and the beauty of it is that although you have survived, there is still space and grace for you to graduate from merely surviving to thriving.

Survival allows you to get through it while thriving speaks to your ability to catapult from it. So, in a sense, it's your pain that has the power to push you into another dimension of possibility.

You just have to choose to let it go.

Examine how holding onto it has affected you. Has it made your life better? More rewarding? Or has it kept you playing small? Has it compelled you to be a victim or a victor?

Your pain does have a purpose, but perhaps it's to elevate you and not break you down. What if the elevation we all desire is wrapped in the tough lessons that we refuse to learn from? What if the next level you desire is on the other side of your pain? Imagine what can happen when you extract the lesson from your pain, learn from it, apply what you've learned to your life, and then reach back and teach someone else how to get through what you've been through?

Isn't this concept a more empowering way to process pain? I know that even my pain has been a profound part of my growth; but it's only when we choose to let go, heal from it, learn from it and decide to be better that we can expect a better life outcome.

Throughout this book, I will share my heart and personal experiences that convey my own childhood trauma, while providing insight on healing techniques, therapeutic practices and even research to inform, equip and inspire your own growth.

This is the critical moment in your life when you can choose to work through you pain. I know it's not the easiest thing to do, but trust me, it's so rewarding. You may feel overwhelmed in the beginning but you are not alone and you are on the right track. It's important to develop a support system and to find a safe space to express yourself as you work on yourself. I would encourage you to find a trusted pastor, hire a therapist, consult with a mentor or someone you trust as you work on yourself. You will need someone to hold you accountable, to listen to you, to provide comfort and someone to push you to continue through when the old you tries to show up and escort you back to your comfort zone.

Take this time now to assess your starting lineup. These people will be the key players throughout your growth journey.

Who will hold you accountable?

_____

_____

_____

_____

_____

_____

_____

_____

Who will provide you with clinical insight?

_____

_____

_____

_____

_____

_____

_____

What resources are available to help you heal and grow?

(search your local directory, are there any free counseling services? Call your current healthcare provider, do they offer mental health counseling as part of your insurance plan? Reach out to HR at your current place of employment, do they offer any mental and emotional health support for their employees? Contact local universities to see if they offer any psychological services for a reduced rate for both students and non students.

_____

_____

_____

_____

_____

_____

_____

Who will encourage and motivate you to be better?

_____

_____

_____

_____

_____

_____

_____

Who will benefit from your healing? Whose life will be better because of your choice to heal?

_____

_____

_____

_____

_____

_____

_____

_____

Taking this journey through healing is so transformative. You deserve to live a life that reflects your hearts desires. Imagine how amazing life can be when your heart is healed?

Now, if you're anything like me, you know that there are some things you need to let go of, but you're just not sure how to do it.

Here are some quick tips to get started as we move on to chapter 2.

1. Create your own mantra to counter painful thoughts of your past.

Growing up, I had this recurring thought that I was worthless, incapable of love and not deserving of having any one stay with me or value my existence. Afterall, my own mother did leave me. Thinking this was so toxic. I had to change my mindset. Establishing a positive mantra that I could repeat daily helped me to do just that.

Whenever thoughts of worthlessness entered my mind, I would immediately check myself and begin to recite my personal mantra.

> "I am whole, I am deserving of love, I am powerful, I am enough. I have always been enough and I will always be enough. Someone's inability to recognize my value does not mean that I don't have any. Because I love myself first, I set the standard. Because I love myself, I recognize real love when it shows up. I can embrace it, I can cherish it, and I can value it because I value myself."

21

You have to examine your own fears and your own pain points. Once you get clear about your fears and shortcomings, you can create a personal mantra that empowers you by countering your negative thoughts.

What are your pain points? Fears? Limitations?

_____

_____

_____

_____

_____

_____

_____

Now what powerful words can you use to replace your negative thoughts? What might you need to affirm to yourself daily to gain strength over disempowering thoughts? Create your own personal mantra.

_____

_____

_____

_____

_____

_____

_____

_____

2. Accept an apology that you may never get.

I know what it feels like to desire closure by way of an apology. I mean, having someone merely acknowledge what they've done to hurt you will be exactly what you need to move on right? In all actuality that's not true at all. Even if they came to you today and offered the apology you've long awaited, what would happen next? You would still need to work through the process of healing. So why not start now?

This is why forgiveness is not for the perpetrator, it's for you. It gives you permission subconsciously to move on. This is why it's not wise to wait for an apology. The sad truth, is that you may never get it, and if you do, the time you spend waiting will be wasted.

3. Surround yourself with people who fill you up. Those who represent the life you are working towards. You need people around you who want to see you win.

Those who fill you up will most likely include those in your starting lineup. Remember, this list should consist of those who compel you to be your best.

Now that you are clear about who will be apart of your support system, Let's focus on next steps.

Forgiving myself was the most life changing thing that I've ever done. I didn't realize how hard I had been on myself. For the longest time, I felt that I was somehow responsible for my abuse. I struggled with knowing exactly where to place blame. This is very common for victims.

> "When you haven't forgiven those
> who've hurt you, you turn your back
> against your future. When you do
> forgive, you start walking forward."
>
> ~ *Tyler Perry*

From a Clinical Perspective: Katherine Wald, LCSW

Licensed psychotherapist and certified EMDR therapist

When working with survivors in my practice, I try to focus on self-forgiveness first. It is important to remember that our body responds to danger in pre-programmed and primitive ways. When faced with real or imagined danger, our body often reacts reflexively with a fight, flight or freeze response. Our body takes in a perceived threat and transmits it to the brain stem. Once the body initiates the freeze response, the parasympathetic nervous system is activated, the heart rate drops, breathing slows down, muscles become limp and endorphins are released, blocking the body's ability to feel pain. This is an automatic and primitive coping response and is not a matter of being emotionally weak. If you were unable to fight off your perpetrator, and did not or could not stop what happened, IT IS NOT YOUR FAULT. It is important that you forgive yourself if you feel guilty about what happened.

Forgiving the perpetrator is another important step you may choose to take. However, it is not necessary in order to heal. Many perpetrators refuse to admit that they have done anything wrong and show little remorse for their actions. Forgiveness does not validate the perpetrator's actions. It does not mean that what the perpetrator did was acceptable or that you should "forget" what happened. Rather, it is an opportunity to let go of some of the power the perpetrator has over you, for you to change your internal response to the event(s) as well as to release some of the anger, rage, fear and obsessive thoughts of revenge that you might have towards the perpetrator.

There are many ways that you can choose to forgive without ever receiving that "apology." You can focus on forgiveness as a way to cope and improve your overall emotional state of being or try to forgive:

- emotionally (by finding compassion for the perpetrator)

- cognitively (in the way that you choose to think about what happened)

- spiritually (by turning to God or to a higher power for help with forgiveness)

Some of the questions you should ask yourself are:

> "How much anger do I still have towards myself for what happened?"

> "What do I need to do to let go and forgive myself?"

> "How do I think forgiving myself can help me to move forward with my life?"

> "Do I want to forgive my abuser? If so, how?"

If you have had more than one abuser, ask yourself these questions about each one. Remember that forgiveness is a process. Be gentle and patient with yourself.

Chapter 2

The *Courage* to Put Myself First

When you have a diminished perspective of your self-worth, you lack a standard to hold others to. When you don't love yourself properly, you give everyone around you permission to do the same. The saying is true, you teach people how to treat you. Can you imagine how hard it is to teach someone something you haven't mastered yourself?

There was a time in my life that I put the needs of everyone before my own. I realize now, that my desperate need to please others was rooted in my fear of rejection. I had developed a fixation on acceptance. In a sense, I felt as if my value was defined by how much others liked me. This way of thinking caused me to go over and beyond to please people. Have you ever found yourself saying yes to things that you know you should be saying no to? Going places you really have no desire to go? Just doing a bunch of stuff to keep everyone happy at the expense of your own happiness?

When you don't really value yourself appropriately, needing validation from others is a comfort that you crave; no matter how uncomfortable it really is.

How many of us put off what we need in order to show up for someone we love? How many of us have actually forgotten what it is that we like?

I found myself feeling extremely burnt out and exhausted from allocating my time, my energy, my focus and my resources towards what everyone else needed from me. The truth of the matter is, I was neglecting myself. It was a behavior I had learned and I had internalized it as acceptable. I mean, I didn't do it on purpose. Deep down, I wanted to be loved, to be valued, and to be put first. However, what I realized, if I didn't put myself first who would? And why would they?

I thought somehow that if I sacrificed myself for others, the reward would be receipt of love that would somehow deem me worthy. What I had to learn was that love and my sense of self-worth would never come from any outside source. No matter how much others loved and appreciated me. The void I was trying to fill was one that had to start from within.

In my mind, like many women who have experienced adoption, abandonment, neglect and even abuse; I had adopted the false idea that I was undeserving. This negative belief was running rampant in my mind, and it showed up in my actions. The proof was in my inability to put myself first.

When you don't prioritize your self-care, you sabotage your ability to experience true fulfillment. When you give all that you have to others, eventually you will have nothing left.

I didn't even realize that I was a people pleaser. If you asked me if I was afraid of not being accepted, I would most likely have been offended by the mere audacity of the question. When I got serious about working on myself, I started to gain the courage to perform a real self-evaluation. I had to come face to face with my bad habits and other things that were contributing to the cycle of frustration, pain and inadequacy in my life.

The good news is that when you gain clarity about the things that are holding you up from experiencing the life that you desire, you can then take action to make the necessary changes to garner more desirable results.

Change can be hard but so is staying stuck in a cycle of habits that keep you living and loving far beneath your potential.

Now don't get me wrong, showing up for others, being dependable, having a heart to help and finding fulfillment in serving the needs of others is not a bad thing. It's just when you do it out of a need for validation, or as a means to receive acceptance that it becomes a toxic trait.

The first question you have to ask yourself is, am I a people pleaser?

Here is a quick checklist to help you determine if you are.

1. You feel responsible for other people's feelings

2. You avoid conflict like the plague

3. You don't admit when your feelings are hurt

4. Saying No is like pulling your own teeth

5. You would rather go with the flow, than say something that could cause even the slightest rift.

6. You are ok with being uncomfortable for the sake of just getting along

7. You find yourself doing A LOT and still not feeling a sense of personal fulfillment.

8. Your to-do list and little to nothing to do with YOU.

9. You would give someone your last, even though YOU NEED IT!

10. You say YES way more often than you say NO!

Next, you have to wonder WHY is it so hard for you to say NO!

1. You fear conflict

2. You don't want to rock the boat

3. You don't want to disappoint anyone

4. You feel a sense of obligation to say yes

5. Saying yes comes naturally to you

6. You think No is negative

7. You don't consider the full extent of the commitment

8. You want to prove your worth

Now that you are clear on why you may struggle with NO, here are some quick tips to help you regain and establish your personal authority.

(How to say No)

Believe it or not, No is a full sentence. You could literally just say NO. You do not have to offer any explanation. Simply saying "NO" is the most effective method. The problem is that most of us dance around the word and consequently end up saying yes. So, practice saying no in the mirror if you need to. Try to avoid apologizing or substituting NO with, "I'm not sure" or "I don't think so". Your ability to say "NO" is your own personal power.

Here are a few alternative ways to say No.

1. "I would love to help you, but I'm unavailable"

2. "I appreciate the gesture but No, thank you"

3. "No Thanks"

4. "I'm honored but I can't"

5. "I'm not able to help"

6. "Thanks for thinking of me but at this time my plate is full"

7. "sounds great, but I can't commit."

8. "It's a great idea, but I'm unable to take on anything else at this time"

9. "I would love to contribute support but my bandwidth is low at the moment"

10. "I try my best to perform in the spirit of excellence, and for that reason I have to limit my commitments."

11. " I don't think I'm a good fit"

12. "My word for the year is yes so I can't fit anything else in"

13. "I'm not able to dedicate the time required."

When you overcommit by saying yes to things that don't serve you, things that don't serve your goals; you waste valuable time and you risk your own fulfillment. Not only do you put your own happiness on the back burner, but you jeopardize your own respect. People tend to respect you more when you stand up for yourself. Plus, when you overcommit you end up being a flake. You only have 24 hours in your day. When you say yes to too many things, you inevitably drop the ball on one or two of them. It's better to say No and save your sanity, than to say yes and risk ruining your reputation. No one wants to be known as the person who doesn't keep their word.

From a Clinical Perspective: Katherine Wald, LCSW

Licensed psychotherapist and certified EMDR therapist

Prioritizing yourself and learning how to say "no" are some of the important components of setting boundaries, which is a critical skill for trauma survivors. Establishing healthy boundaries is necessary for forming and sustaining mental, physical, emotional, and spiritual health, and is an important part of the healing process. Understanding boundary violations that have occurred in your life, how they have impacted you, and how healthy boundaries are set moving forward can transform your relationship with yourself and others.

Skin is an example of a physical boundary that protects the body. Think about what happens if you get a large scratch; your body can become susceptible to infection. The same is true when your emotional and relational boundaries are violated; you can become vulnerable to harm and your internal sense of safety can feel compromised. Let's explore different types of boundaries that trauma survivors might struggle with and the ways in which you can set limits to protect yourself.

Physical boundaries

It is important for you to identify the amount of physical space that you need around others in order to feel comfortable. Ask yourself the following questions:

- How close is too close for my comfort?

- If someone gets too close, what do I do? How do I feel?

- Are there current situations or circumstances where I find people getting physically too close to me? If so, who are they and how do I react?

- Can I be assertive and maintain my personal space if someone invades it?

- What is my definition of unwelcome physical contact?

- How do I react if someone violates my physical boundary by:

  o Standing too close to me
  o Brushing their body up against mine
  o Touching me in a nonsexual way if I have no desire to be touched
  o Touching me in a sexual way when I do not want to be touched
  o Hits, grabs, pushes, or kicks me
  o Gets in my face and talks too close

Setting limits verbally can be difficult, especially when you are first learning how to set boundaries. A good way to start is by using your body language and facial expressions to convey the message "back off" or "come closer to me." For example, if you want to communicate to someone that you want them to "back off" you can:

- Cross your arms over your chest

- Turn your body away from the person

- Move your head in the other direction if someone is talking or standing too close to you

- Glare at the person in an unfriendly manner

On the other hand, if you want someone to "come closer" you can also use body language and facial expressions. For example:

- Make eye contact

- Smile

- Move physically closer to the other person

Think about the ways in which your physical boundaries have been violated and how you can use body language to create and maintain good physical boundaries for yourself.

If using body language does not work, think of things you can do or say to protect yourself from further violations. One of my favorite interpersonal techniques for effectively setting boundaries, resolving conflict, and respectfully making a request is the Dialectical

Behavioral Therapy (DBT) skill, DEAR MAN. Each letter in DEAR MAN is an acronym representing its own skill.

The "D" stands for describe. First you want to describe the situation in the simplest way you can. Here you are only stating the facts of what is bothering you without getting into feelings or anything else. For example, "When we sit down to watch television at night, I notice that you have been putting your hand on my upper thigh."

The "E" stands for express. This is where you express your feelings about the situation. Try to use "I" statements, not "you" statements here to convey how you feel impacted by the other person's behavior or actions. For example, "I feel very uncomfortable when you put your hand there as it reminds me of how my brother used to initiate sexual contact with me when we were little."

The "A" stands for assert. This is where you assert yourself and ask for what you want or say no. For example, "I prefer it if you do not touch my upper thigh, since that area of my body is a big trigger for me."

The "R" stands for reinforce. Here you can "reward" positive behavior and even improve the relationship. For example, "If you are able to remember that this part of my body is off limits, I will feel so much more comfortable and relaxed sitting next to you, and will be more open to other kinds of physical contact in the future."

The "M" stands for (stay) mindful, which means staying present in the here and now. Do not get sidetracked by bringing up past grievances. Stay focused in the moment and the current issue you are trying to address. If the other person becomes defensive or tries to distract away from the situation, you can try using the "broken record" technique. This technique essentially consists of you formulating a short, specific, easy to understand statement about what you want, and repeating this statement as many times as necessary, like a broken record, until the other person gets the message. For example:

> You: When you put your hand on my upper thigh, it makes me feel very uncomfortable. I would like for you to not touch me there when I sit next to you.

> Other person: Stop trying to tell me what to do all the time. It's always something. I can never do anything right with you.

> You: Touching me on my upper thigh makes me uncomfortable and I would like it to stop.

> Other person: Oh geez! Stop being such a drama queen. What's the big deal? I'm just trying to be affectionate and here you go again icing me out.

> You: Touching me on my upper thigh reminds me of things in my past, it makes me uncomfortable, and I need it to stop.

Other person: Ok fine. Is touching you on your arm ok?

You: Yes, and thank you for asking.

The second "A" stands for appear confident. Keep your head up, shoulders back, and maintain eye contact when communicating. Speak in a calm, clear and loud voice. When you appear confident, people will take you more seriously and it will be easier to enforce your boundaries.

Lastly, the "N" stands for negotiate. Remember you are not demanding anything. You are asking for something. Be willing to give in order to get. Try to figure out a solution that is agreeable to both parties involved.

Emotional Boundaries

Having emotional boundaries allows you to set limits without being afraid that you are upsetting or disappointing others. Being able to ask for what you want and deserve, realizing that you have a right to say "no", and setting limits without the fear that you will be abandoned or hurt is an essential part of being able to establish good emotional boundaries.

An effective way of creating and maintaining good boundaries is to create your own "bill of rights." For example:

- I have the right to choose with whom and when I want to be sexual

- I have the right to turn down sex (even with my partner)

- I have the right to my own personal space (and keep others out)

- I have the right to say "no" and not feel guilty

Think of the examples above. How do they make you feel? What emotions do you experience when you think about each one of these examples? What happens to you when you try to assert yourself in that way? Do you believe you have the right to these boundaries? If no, why? If yes, why? Think about creating your own "bill of rights." What would you like yours to say?

Remember, as the poet Robert Frost famously wrote: "good fences make good neighbors." Maintaining healthy boundaries is an essential part of your healing process.

Chapter 3

Nothing to Hide

"Devotion requires a willingness, openness and readiness to embrace the truth. It is a process of opening yourself to receive what already is. God's goodness and love already exist. God's love leads us to the truth."

~ Iyanla Vanzant

Most of my personal development occurred after I became very honest with myself. When I courageously sat with thoughts that had previously tormented me, I became more aware of just how profound being honest with myself really was. The truth can be traumatic and downright scary but it's the most frightening thing that will ever set you free. You see, truth can hurt you but if you embrace it, it will heal you.

The reason why people avoid truth is because it exposes things that we want to keep hidden; It sheds light on dark places and it digs up the dirtiest of demons that we'd otherwise like to keep buried. The problem with hiding, covering, concealing and burying our truth, is that it takes up space in our hearts and minds and it stunts our growth.

Although speaking and standing in our personal truth is liberating, it's not always the easiest thing to do. Especially when doing so can have life altering effects.

I remember waking up one morning with my pajama pants and underwear removed. I knew that my young body had been violated the night before, but the initial shock of it all left me paralyzed in fear. That morning proved to be the first of many. Eventually, I would learn to redress my small frame after each assault.

Although I would rise the next morning with my underwear back in place, they were soaked in urine from my traumatized bladder emptying itself in what I now know to be a symptom of abuse and a sign of childhood sexual abuse.

Research shows that one in four girls will be sexually abused before they turn 18 years old. Only 12% of child sexual abuse is reported. (National Sexual Violence Resource Center 2012, 2013, 2015.) There are so many contributing factors to this phenomenon.

1. They may have been taught to obey adults and to not question their authority

2. They have been threatened to keep quiet

3. They have promised to keep the assault a secret

4. They have been bribed into secrecy

5. They feel guilty and believe that the abuse is their fault

6. They are ashamed

7. They are too young to understand that the abuse is inappropriate and even criminal

8. They don't have the vocabulary or know the words to use to tell.

I remember when I finally opened up to my adoptive mother about the sexual abuse I endured during my stay in foster care. It had taken every bit of courage my young mind could muster up, to finally speak up. Her response was almost as devastating as the actual offense. I can't say whether or not she believed me, because she literally didn't say or do anything about it. Looking back, I can understand the fear of facing such a hard truth. In fact, avoidance of the catastrophic consequences and aftermath of exposing offenders has been one of the greatest contributing factors to unreported abuse.

Often times the offender is someone close to the family or even worse, a part of the family. This is often the case because close family and friends typically have access.

Finally speaking out, and then having the abuse silenced made me feel as though what had happened to me was not a big deal. Even though it caused me to have spells where I would wet the bed, it led to promiscuity, a sex addiction, and even sexual misconduct as a kid; I had internalized the events as insignificant while the effects of it damaged me mentally, emotionally and spiritually.

At the tender age of 8 I was already engaging in masturbation. Being introduced to sexual behavior so young resulted in increased curiosity in touch and feel sensational interest in my body.

I was confused about what was appropriate and normal for my age. My innocence had been taken; my mind was perverted, and I had been robbed of my purity.

This is common for children who experience sexual abuse.

Let's explore some common signs and symptoms of childhood sexual abuse.

From a Clinical Perspective:
Katherine Wald, LCSW

Licensed psychotherapist and certified EMDR therapist

There are many signs and symptoms of childhood sexual abuse. It's important to know what to look for, what to do, and how to respond if you suspect that a child is being abused.

*SIGNS OF SEXUAL ABUSE IN CHILDREN

Physical warning signs:

- Sexually transmitted infections (STIs)

- Signs of trauma to the genital area, unexplained bleeding, bruising, burning while urinating, blood on the bed sheets or underwear

Behavioral warning signs:

- Sexual behavior that is inappropriate for the child's age (i.e. poor body boundaries and/or inappropriate touching of others in their private areas)

- Bedwetting or soiling the bed, even into adolescence and early adulthood

- Not wanting to be left alone with certain people or being afraid to be away from primary caregivers (especially if this is a new behavior)

- Attempts to avoid having to remove clothing, even to change or bathe

- Refusing to bathe or bathing excessively

- Using language that is "too adult" for the child's age

- Behavioral changes like suddenly becoming less talkative or isolating self from others

- Shrinking away from physical contact, suddenly not wanting to be touched or hugged

- Fear of bathrooms

Emotional Signs:

- Inordinate amount of talk about or knowledge of sexual topics

- Regressive behavior, such as resuming behaviors that the child might have previously outgrown (i.e. thumbsucking)

- Frequent nightmares, night terrors, and/or fear of being alone at night

- Excessive worry and/or fearfulness

- Withdrawing into themselves and isolating from others

- Increase in restlessness, difficulty concentrating, and/or suddenly becoming more demanding

- Older children might also begin to act out, become angry and oppositional, engage in numbing behaviors such as drug and alcohol use or self-mutilation (i.e. cutting)

*EFFECTS OF SEXUAL ABUSE

Common feelings
related to abuse and its aftereffects:

- Guilt and responsibility

- Shame

- Anger

- Fear

- Confusion

- Depression

- Low self-esteem

- Lack of sense of self

- Trust issues

- Feelings of being "different"

- Feelings of isolation or wanting to withdraw from others

- Feelings that you were never a child

<u>Common Symptoms related to abuse:</u>

- Sexual problems (acting out, aversion to, or absence of feelings)

- Body memories (physical re-experiencing of traumatic events)

- Nightmares and night terrors

- Flashbacks/disturbing thoughts

- Suicide attempts

- Body mutilation such as burning or cutting

- Eating disorders/body image distortions

- History of exploitative/abusive adult relationships

- Alcohol or drug use/abuse

- Parenting difficulties

- Difficulties with being assertive

- Abusive behaviors towards others

- Excessive caretaking of others

- Emotional outbursts

- Inability to see many positives or strengths in oneself

- Physical health problems due to stress on the body

- Phobias, panic/anxiety attacks

- Problematic interpersonal relationships, especially intimate relationships

- Lack of or gaps in memories of childhood

- Dissociation/disconnecting from surroundings, feelings, memories, actions, or the body

- Hypervigilance (feeling on edge/high alert)

*WAYS TO PREVENT SEXUAL ABUSE

There are no foolproof ways to prevent child sexual abuse. However, there are things you can do to reduce the risk:

- Try to stay involved in your children's lives and ask about their day-to-day activities. Know what games they played at recess, who sat with them at lunch, which friends are being mean and who is being nice, ask what they did during the day and who they did it with. The more involved you are in your children's lives, the more clearly you can see the warning signs if something is different or "off" with your children. It will also allow your children to feel more comfortable talking to you about things. Get to know who they hang out with (including other children and adults). Ask about teammates, coaches, parents of friends, and older siblings of classmates that they might be spending time with. Create an open dialogue about these people and ask questions so that your children feel comfortable sharing with you.

- Choose carefully who you let your children spend time with. Thoroughly screen babysitters, nannies, after school mentors, and others who spend significant time around your children.

- Familiarize yourself with the warning signs of sexual abuse and pay attention to any changes in your children's behavior. If you notice anything that does not feel right, address it immediately.

- Talk to your children about abuse. Sexual violence, especially since the "Me Too" movement, is increasingly being portrayed on the news and on television. Use this as an opportunity to start a conversation with your children. You can ask questions like, "If you were in a situation like this, what do you think you would do?" or "Have you ever heard of things like this happening before? What have you heard?" Children will often emulate their parents. Try to cultivate a home that feels safe, open and honest as a model for your children.

- Encourage your children to express themselves when something doesn't feel right. Reassure them that they will be taken seriously. You can start these conversations as soon as your children are old enough to use words that express feelings or emotions.

- Teach your children about boundaries. Especially body boundaries and which parts of their bodies are "private." You can talk about "good touch" and "bad touch." Let your child know that nobody has the right to touch them in a way that feels uncomfortable. This even includes family members. It is important for them to learn that their body is their own and that no one has the right to touch them if they do not want to be touched. Even if Grandpa is tickling and hugging them, and they do not like it, they have every right to tell Grandpa to stop and to inform another adult if their boundaries are being ignored.

- From an early age, make sure to teach your children about their body parts and the names of those parts. Giving your children this vocabulary allows them the ability to verbalize to you more effectively if something does not feel right.

- Try to set aside alone time with your children where they can have your undivided attention. Let them know that no matter what, they can talk to you if they have questions, if someone is making them uncomfortable, or if they just need time to talk or vent. If your children come to you with questions or concerns, make sure you follow through on your word and set aside a special time just for them.

- **Let your children know they will not get into trouble if they share information with you.** Perpetrators often use threats, keeping secrets, and other forms of manipulation to keep children from disclosing the abuse. Remind your children that no matter what has happened or what they need to tell you, they will not get into trouble by being honest. Make sure you follow through on your promises. If your children do come to you, be sure to express your pride in their courage for speaking up rather than punishing them for it no matter what they say.

- Allow your children the space to address things with you on your own. Many times direct questions such as "How was school?" and "Was practice fun?" may not give you accurate or detailed answers. Instead try to give your children a platform to address whatever concerns they might be having on their own. You can do this by asking open-ended questions, like "Is there anything else that happened today?" or "Is there anything else you wanted to talk to me about?"

- It is important to be validating not dismissive or minimizing when children come to you with a problem. Saying things like "come on, that's not a big deal" or "be a big boy and don't cry" cause children to feel invalidated, and will make them less likely to come to you in the future if they have a problem.

*HOW TO START A CONVERSATION WITH SOMEONE YOU SUSPECT MAY BE GETTING ABUSED

- Find a non-threatening environment where you think the child might feel comfortable opening up to you, and a time and place when you can talk to the child alone. Make sure you find a place that is quiet and private where you won't be interrupted by others.

- Be mindful of the tone of voice that you use and your body language. Try to make the conversation feel comfortable and use a calm, non-threatening tone.

- Ask open-ended questions so that you do not lead the child and can elicit accurate responses (not just what the child thinks you want to hear). Use language that the child can understand. Remember that sexual abuse does not always physically "hurt" so steer clear of questions like "is anyone 'hurting' you." Instead you can ask a series of questions. For example, you can say something like, "I notice that you haven't seemed like yourself lately. Has anything been bothering you?" Or "I notice that you have not been playing with your friends. I wonder how you have been feeling recently?" It is important not to make assumptions or to push a child to talk if they are not ready. You want to create an atmosphere where the child feels safe to open up.

- **DO NOT LEAD THE CHILD!!!** Questions like, "Does your daddy ever touch your vagina" is an example of leading the child. This can affect police proceedings, court cases, and most importantly the child's own account of events. It can even create false memories. Open-ended questions are always best. Some examples of open-ended questions that would be helpful are, "Is there someone doing something to you that makes you feel afraid?" or "Is there anyone doing things with you that make you feel uncomfortable?"

- Follow up on any comments or behaviors that seem like they are not age appropriate. Ask the child "Where did you learn that? Did someone tell you that or did you see that somewhere?" This can open up a conversation about what has been happening with the child. Again be mindful of your tone of voice. Do not get angry or make the child feel like they did something wrong or are in trouble. Just be curious, calm, and open.

- Avoid judgment and blame. Reassure the child they are not in trouble. Try to use "I" statements rather than "You" statements. For example, "I am concerned that I heard you say that Daddy comes into your bed in the middle of the night and Mommy doesn't know."

*NEXT STEPS AFTER THE DISCOVERY OF ABUSE

Before you report

- Tell the child that you are going to talk to someone who can help. Be clear that this is not up for debate or that you are asking them for permission. The child might be frightened and beg you not to tell, especially if the perpetrator threatened them, their loved ones or is a family member themselves. Remind the child (and yourself) that you need to keep the child safe and by reporting you are doing just that.

- Make sure the child is in a safe place. If the abuse is happening in the child's home, do not let the child return home. If you are not concerned about the parents causing the child harm, consult with the parents about what the child has disclosed to you.

- If you are concerned about the child's safety, or if you think the perpetrator might retaliate upon learning about the investigation, make sure you let the authorities know this when you report.

Where to report:

- **Reporting can be made anonymously.** If you suspect child abuse or mistreatment, call your State's Child Protective Services. As long as there is suspicion of abuse and it is being done in good faith, a report should be made, even if you do not have definite proof. It is not your job to investigate. Leave that to the authorities.

- Reporting agencies vary from state to state, but you can go to RAINN (Rape, Abuse, & Incest

National Network) www.RAINN.org and search their State Law Database to find where you can report in your state. You can also call or text the National Child Abuse Hotline at: 800-422-4453, where you can talk to a trained volunteer who can walk you through the reporting process, and tell you what to expect. The hotline volunteer can guide you, but cannot file a report for you.

No More Shame!

As I got older, I kept quiet about my assault. I didn't talk about it, sometimes I didn't even think about it, but somehow it kept showing up in my life. It showed up in the men that I dated, it showed up in my unstable lifestyle, and it showed up in my diminished self-esteem.

I felt so ashamed, like I was damaged goods. I felt guilty for the secrets I was keeping and I was embarrassed about the disgusting things that happened to me.

Do you ever feel bad about your abuse? Do you struggle with feelings of self blame?

_____

_____

_____

_____

_____

_____

_____

_____

_____

_____

_____

_____

_____

_____

Take a moment to think, are feelings of shame causing you to avoid talking about or working through your abuse?

_____

_____

_____

_____

_____

_____

_____

_____

_____

From a Clinical Perspective: Katherine Wald, LCSW

Licensed psychotherapist and certified EMDR therapist

Every survivor I have worked with has struggled to some degree with feelings of shame. With shame, there is a deep sense that "there is something wrong with me." Many times there is even an irrational feeling that the survivor somehow caused the abuse. It is important to note that in my over 15 years in practice, I have never met a single survivor who was to blame for their abuse.

Many times a survivor's body can respond to sexual stimulation with a degree of pleasure, even if what is happening is emotionally repulsive. Survivors can also possess confusing feelings towards their perpetrator, mistaking the abuse for love or even enjoying the feeling of being "special." This can contribute to feelings that the abuse was somehow "my fault," which cannot be further from the truth. It is never ok for a person who is more powerful to take advantage of a person's vulnerability, curiosity, innocence, or need to feel loved. Abuse is never the fault of the vulnerable. Rather, the full responsibility falls on the more powerful person in the equation.

Before you let go of shame, you have to understand it, label it, and acknowledge it. When you hold in secrets and keep those feelings inside, shame only grows bigger and has more and more power over you. Admitting shame is the first step toward taking back control and lessening its power. Some ways you can do this is by identifying some of the reasons that you might be blaming yourself for what happened to you. Review your answers and try to dispute those reasons. You can then come up with some positive affirmations that you can say to yourself instead of the messages of shame and self-loathing that you might be carrying. For example: "I deserve to be treated with consideration and respect."

Another thing you can try is to look at children who are the same age that you were at the time of your abuse. Notice how vulnerable and innocent they are. Is it realistic to blame a child that age for not stopping the abuse? Look at how big they are physically. Asking a child to stop a more powerful person from abusing them would be like asking a rabbit to try to fend off a lion. Can you see how easy it would be to manipulate a child at the same age you were when you were abused? If you found out that one of the children you are watching was being abused, do you think that it would be their fault? The same logic applies to you.

Chapter 4

Triggered

"Avoiding triggers isn't healing. Healing happens when you are triggered and you are able to move through the pain, the pattern and the story and walk your way towards a different ending."

~ Vienna Pharaoh

Chaotic silence is the best way that I can describe the moment when I realized just how much my childhood experiences had emotionally held me captive to a cycle of dysfunction.

Perhaps it was the lies that I knew he was feeding me that triggered my frustration with having to dance outside of the truth. I was so sick and tired of having to avoid facts in order to comfort someone else's ego or their refusal to face the truth. I had always struggled to cultivate close relationships. All of my interactions and engagements with men were surface level. I had built a wall to protect myself from the possibility of being hurt by anyone. If I kept everyone outside of my wall, they couldn't get close enough to my heart to hurt me or disappoint me. He was the first man that I had allow myself to love without limits. He was the one who I loved without conditions. I saw something in him that I wanted to heal, he had faced some brokenness in his life as well, but he was willing to grow. Loving him gave me purpose. As I loved him I was able to witness his growth. It's crazy how much tender love and genuine care can help someone transform. I watched him learn to eat better, and evolve in a way that he had always wanted to. I had given him my love, my support and my energy. I gave him the love I had always hoped someone would give to me. So, when we started to face conflict in our relationship, when I felt like he wasn't being open and honest at times, I started to retreat emotionally. I remember feeling so uncomfortable and vulnerable. I couldn't really figure out why small conflicts and disagreements would stir up massive amounts of emotions. It hit mid argument and I froze with the awakening that my fear of feeling not heard, not valued and silenced triggered my childhood emotional injuries.

As a kid, my brothers and I were forced to lie about, and keep quiet about things that in normal circumstances would never warrant a cover story.

We weren't able to tell anyone that we were adopted; we couldn't speak about the abuse that we had endured or the living conditions we were suffering through. Nothing was to be disclosed. Any punishment, conversation or situation that happened was to be kept tight lipped. We lived under the "what goes on in this house, stays in this house" rule and we were upholding one of the longest standing, toxic behavior patterns of generations.

Keeping secrets was something that I had learned early on. It always made me feel trapped on the inside. Like the real me, was hiding in a shell and if I ever revealed my true self, my fragile cover would shatter. Truth was that thing that would cause everything to break. So, I concealed secrets in order to prevent chaos.

This was a technique that I had mastered as a young girl. It was a part of my survival guide. Keeping quiet profited me a false sense of outer peace, but it cost me years of inner suffering. I had learned to wear a mask. I had become an expert in looking good on the outside as a distraction to cover my brokenness inside. As I grew up, I learned to push through my pain by ignoring it all together. It wasn't until I fell in love as an adult that I discovered how much I was triggered by secrets. I had moved on to build a life for myself by detaching from anything that reminded me of my childhood. Or at least that was what I thought. When my relationship got rocky, I felt so vulnerable that I had to assess my fears. I wanted to understand the root of my discomfort. I mean, any woman would have some level of uneasiness if she felt that she was losing her sense of security in her relationship. This type of response is quite normal when you look at it from that standpoint. When I examined the root cause of my anxieties, painful memories from my childhood resurfaced. I was reminded of all the things that I had held in. I realized how much I craved security and stability as an adult.

Finding comfort in my relationship provided a sense of safety for me. It felt like the love that I had always wanted. It was my first long term relationship and the concept of someone staying with me was the only standard I had in place to evaluate someone's love for me. It was as if staying was enough.

I had put up with things that should have made me walk away. I had forgiven offenses that grudged my heart; I learned the worst parts of love and how when you fail to love yourself first you allowed someone else to set the standard. When you love yourself the least, you hurt yourself the most. When you lack the ability to experience love first hand, you give someone else the role of loving you and completing you, when self-love is your responsibility. So, staying with me while also tremendously feeding dysfunction in my life didn't seem like such a bad deal.

I kept telling myself that my situation wasn't that bad. The problem was that I was craving a life that was great. So even if the situation wasn't "that bad", it still wasn't good enough for me. For once in my life, I was so sick and tired of making the best out of a bad situation. What I wanted more than anything was to know what it felt like to be better. I had accepted brokenness in my life for so long. I couldn't help but wonder what it would feel like to finally heal. I wondered what my life could be like if I didn't allow my fear of rejection and abandonment to show up and sabotage the good things that were sprouting in my life.

Avoiding conversations and thoughts that created conflict had allowed me to survive my childhood, but that way of coping was not effective as a grown woman. I learned to honor my feelings by having the courage to allow myself to simply be in the moment, and process the emotions that were stirring inside. Doing so helped me to see how my old fears were showing up in my new life. Learning to work through my feelings gave me deeper insight and a greater understanding of my personal limitations. This was life changing. When I discovered my limitations, I realized what I needed help with and what I needed to work on. Having an awakening to the things that are blocking your true-life fulfillment can be your greatest weapon when you develop the courage to work on yourself.

One of the most important things you can work on is understanding the areas where you are weak. When you know your weaknesses, you can be intentional about doing the work required to fortify strength in that area. For me, it was recovering from emotional scars. Making the decision to go to therapy, finding a church home that could feed me reminders of God's grace in my life, and finally doing the hard work to remove ineffective coping mechanisms and replacing them with behaviors that would offer me better results. Like gaining a better understanding of myself and sweeping the debris of delinquent disaster out of my life and not just under the rug. Sweeping things under the rug only hides what needs to be cleaned up, it doesn't get rid of it.

Take this time to think of negative patterns that keep showing up in your life.

What is the recurring theme of your conflicts?

_____

_____

_____

_____

_____

_____

_____

_____

_____

_____

What thoughts are governing your beliefs? Habits and behaviors?

_____

_____

_____

_____

_____

_____

_____

_____

_____

What is your "go-to" response to resolve conflict? How do you respond to trouble in your life? Do you avoid it? Do you shut down? Think of the last time you faced something difficult. Was your method effective?

_____

_____

_____

_____

_____

_____

_____

_____

_____

_____

_____

_____

Recognizing Your triggers.

What were the situations and circumstances that led to your last conflict. Reflect and assess the underlying fear that was fueling your frustration. We are all triggered by different things. It's important to be able to identify the things that spark your negative emotions so that you can be intentional about gaining power of them. For me, it was the presence of inconsistency in my relationship. For you it could be maintaining friendships with people who don't honor your growth, staying in an environment that you can't grow in, hanging on to habits that continue to garner the same results or refusing to forgive, forget and truly let go. No matter what it is that you are struggling with, have the courage to take a look at it and be wise enough to implement a weapon to help you win against it.

Your triggers represent your RED zone. This is where you establish boundaries by redlining anything, any person, any behavior, any belief or any habit that puts you at an increased likelihood of reverting back to any self sabotaging ways. Write out a list of anything that happened in your history that is a threat to your destiny.

Identify behaviors, situations, people and places that have the capabilities to onset painful memories.

_____

_____

_____

_____

_____

_____

_____

_____

_____

_____

_____

_____

Now I want you to dream a little. Now that you have your list of triggers, fears and self limiting beliefs, I want you to create a new list that represents the possibilities in your life. This list should include all the things you do well. All the people who inspire you to be better. It can be a close friend, a colleague or a mentor who can provide you with the right amount of motivation to take action. Be sure to include the self care practices that replenish you and anything else that fills you up.

Now that you have both lists, I want you to draw a red line through everything that you have written on your red zone list. This is a visual representation of what you must eliminate out of your life. You have to literally stop doing the things that bring you negative results. Stopping a bad habit tends to be easier when you have something to replace it with. Now, look at your green list. Draw a circle around everything you have written in green. This exercise helps you to literally draw a circle around the things that you need to focus on. Green represents what you should give your time, energy and focus to. Work on eliminating and crossing out the things that drain you and being more intentional about working on what inspires you.

Create a safe zone to help you cope with triggers.

_____

_____

_____

_____

_____

_____

_____

From a Clinical Perspective:
Katherine Wald, LCSW

Licensed psychotherapist and certified EMDR therapist

A key aspect of helping yourself move through the trauma you experienced is learning how to tolerate difficult emotions and triggers without needing to hurt yourself or try to "numb" the pain of the memories. Identifying what your triggers are and then working on ways to move yourself through them can give you control and power over these emotions. Once you know what your triggers are, you can also come up with a game plan to help you dull the intensity of those overwhelming emotions. For example, if your abuser smelled like a specific beer, you can force yourself to open up a bottle of that beer and smell it until that smell is no longer triggering. As an anger release, you can then choose to smash the bottle against the ground. Another exercise you can try is combining a new activity that you enjoy, and incorporating some aspect of your trigger into the activity. That way you can transform the trigger into something that has a positive association. For example, if touching a certain part of your body is a trigger, experiment by having your partner slowly and gently trace around that area with their fingertips while you watch your favorite movie. It is important with this exercise, like all touch exercises, that you communicate clearly with your partner when you need to stop and that you approach this exercise gradually.

Exploring your triggers can be a difficult and painful process. Internally you might want to avoid dealing with your triggers or facing the hurt altogether. Remind yourself that as painful as this process may be, identifying triggers and then working through them is a necessary step towards healing. Establishing a game plan and sticking to that plan over time will result in emotional triggers having less and less power over you. If you feel like you cannot address difficult memories and emotions directly, use any other form of expression such as poetry, art, music, dance, photography, journaling, or making a collage to process your emotions. The key is to face your triggers, understand them, then move through the pain of your memories so that you can move forward in life. Remember, this takes time, so it is important to be patient with yourself as you work on your triggers. Change doesn't happen overnight. Try to work a little on your triggers every day until they lessen their intensity. Think of three actions you can take that might help you to control each of your triggers. Now you have a game plan!

Chapter 5

Graced to Grow

"When you begin to realize that your past does not necessarily dictate the outcome of your future, then you can release the hurt. It is impossible to inhale new air until you exhale the old"

~ Bishop T.D Jakes

None of us are exempt from experiencing some trouble in our lives. No matter where you are on your journey, what your social status is, how many commas you have in your bank account, or where you come from; we are all having a human experience and that alone comes with inevitable suffering at some point and of some sort.

While we all have to fight our own unique battles, there is an immeasurable amount of grace that showers us in the midst of our storms.

What I know for sure, is that storms always pass. They never stay. Storms are a natural yet temporary phenomenon. Storms come, they shake things up yet nourish at the same time. After the storm passes, the ground is ripe for growth but there may be things that have broken along its path.

Much like the storms in your life, difficult moments come but they don't stay. Each trying moment in your life has been a divine lesson to teach you and refine you.

While hard moments bring discomfort, they offer the gift of growth. Pain hurts, but it also prepares us for what's next in our lives.

People tend to despise discomfort because it forces you to adjust. There's no way to grow without change, and change requires work. You cannot reach new heights when you are committed to staying where you are. Work is glamorized but also dreaded. Everyone falls in love with the idea of success but turn around and dread the execution and the effort necessary to achieve it.

When I got sick and tired of revolving issues tripping me up in life, I had to work to make life altering changes. I had to work on my mindset. I had to work to change my perspective on how I saw myself. I had to do the inner work to remove emotional bandaids that I had applied in order to self soothe and hide my wounds.

When I made the decision to hire a therapist in order to finally peel back the layers of my suffering, I had to give myself permission to release all the heaviness of guilt, shame, fear, doubt, brokenness, and any other issue I had allowed to dictate my identity. Time was up for settling and suffering. I was completely done with hiding behind my hurt and masking the parts of me that I didn't want anyone to see.

I had to learn how to view myself from a brand new perspective. There was a time in my life when I truly believed that I possessed no beauty. It was hard to find something that I liked about myself. Being taunted by demeaning name calling didn't help. The danger in being called names by someone who is supposed to love and uphold you is that when you're a kid, you're vulnerable and more likely to believe the untruths about who you are.

The hardest part of the process was working to develop a healthy mindset, and allowing myself to be placed in positions that were conducive for real growth. This required me to get uncomfortable. The areas in my life that needed the most growth, were the same areas that I had always avoided. It was the broken parts of me that I had always covered up. When I unveiled the broken little girl that was living inside my shell of an adult, I came face to face with the root cause of my fears. The same fears that ruled my life as a young girl were still dominating my adult life.

When I examined the pain of my past, I made a conscious decision that I no longer wanted to stunt my growth by having a limited vision of myself. I looked at my reflection in the mirror one day, and I reminded myself that I was no longer a young girl who had no voice to speak up about her abuse. I was no longer that young girl who had to keep secrets to protect the reputation of individuals who had violated me. I was no longer that young girl who was blind to her own beauty and unable to recognize her own worth.

I was finally able to see myself, and not for what I had been through, but for who I was and what I had survived. This is when I graduated from a victim to a survivor. Gaining the courage to share my story and help others break free from the chains of their own trauma allowed me to further elevate from a survivor to an advocate.

Now when I look over my life, I no longer question why God allowed certain things happen to me. I see now, how all of it has worked in divine order to bring me to this exact place in my life where I can now operate in and produce purpose. Had I not been afflicted, abandoned, molested, mentally abused, mistreated and mishandled, then I would lack the qualification to help others grow through these same pain points. It's hard to help someone grow through a situation that you yourself have never been in. When I started to shift the way I viewed my history, I became empowered to create and live a more powerful future.

You deserve an opportunity to do the same. You can't wait for anyone to give you permission to level up. This is an inner green light that you have to activate on your own.

What old beliefs about your potential or your worth are sabotaging your happiness?

Do you still see yourself from the perspective of your pain?

When a traumatic event shakes up your childhood, it can leave you scarred. Perhaps you are still living with the after effects of your own childhood emotional injury.

Are your current habits, beliefs and self talk driven by your fears and insecurities?

Take this time to get clear about where you may need to focus on personal development.

Is it self esteem?

Is it your confidence?

Is it setting healthy boundaries?

Is it learning how to say no?

Is it learning how to move on?

It is learning how to forgive yourself?

Sometimes looking back helps you to get a better view of what's ahead.

Reflect on what bruised you so that you can figure out where you need to build. I was broken emotionally, so I became very intentional about healing my sense of self worth.

Give yourself the grace to grow by confronting your fears, learning healthy ways to cope with your triggers and giving yourself as many second chances as you need to get it right.

You don't get to grow without experiencing some sort of growing pains. Give yourself permission to feel uncomfortable, to make some mistakes along the way or to get it wrong without feeling like a failure. Chances are, you aren't failing you are simply growing. You are learning brand new ways to live a better life, brand new ways to overcome opposition and brand new ways to love yourself better. If ever you falter, guess what? You can get back up again. If ever you get off track, you can get back in line. This is why forgiveness is so important, because when you learn to forgive others, it becomes so much easier to forgive yourself.

Chapter 6

The courage to be better

"When the goal in front of you
becomes more powerful than the
obstacle behind you, you
will always win"
~ *Bishop T.D Jakes*

The best thing you can do after you've been abused, broken, misunderstood and mishandled is to become better instead of broken. Change the way you view your situation. If you see yourself as a victim, you will always be just that; but when you begin to develop a new and improved vision for yourself, you open up your mind to more possibilities.

The hardest part about growth is that when your life begins to expand, you have to be able to change your method. You can't move forward when you're applying an old formula to a new level in your life.

I had always coped with my trauma by just pushing past it, I always expected people to disappoint me and to hurt me, and guess what, they always did. When I started to work on my mind, I developed a healthier perspective. I learned to lead with love instead of fear. I learned to stop expecting the worst outcome and to allow more hope and optimism to govern my day. When I made that shift, more and more good things started to manifest in my life. This was in large part due to the fact that I started to expect goodness, grace, growth, healing, love, purpose and happiness and because I expected it, it showed up.

Working on myself was one of the best decisions I ever made. I started to surround myself with good people. Those who were grateful, inspired, dreaming, building, growing; those who were happy. Those operating in their purpose and those who were focused on making an impact. When I did this, it inspired me to take a deeper look at my life. When I looked over my life, I started to feel a sense of responsibility. I thought about my upbringing and all the days and nights I cried. I thought about my upbringing and all the painful experiences that I had survived. That's when it dawned on me. Yes, I had gone through things that no child should ever have to live through, but despite how hurtful the experiences may have been, I lived, I learned and I had survived. I started to feel more and more compelled to tell my story. I started to discover how purpose could be extracted from my pain. I wanted to use my experiences to help someone else. I wanted to use my voice to let children who have been abused, neglected, abandoned and mishandled to know that nothing that they have been through had the power to diminish their worth. It took me years to come to this understanding. Years of poor coping, bad relationships, negative habits and many rock bottom moments to truly understand that my worth was not determined by people who were unable, unwilling or incapable of recognizing and honoring my greatness. Their inability to see it or celebrate it did not mean that it did not exist.

Self esteem starts with "self". I had to love myself, honor myself and put myself first. I committed to the work required to see myself healed and whole. I knew that it was important for me to see it first, because you cannot be what you cannot see.

I started to look at myself in the mirror each day and compliment myself. I stopped waiting on others to validate me when I finally learned how to love myself. When you really love yourself, you take better care of yourself. You eat right, you take time to work out, you release people who make you feel bad about yourself and you become empowered to say no to and walk away from things that don't make you better.

Not only did I want to live a better life, but I felt a strong conviction to contribute to the world at large. I wanted to do something that would really help others.

I know all too well what it feels like to be on the receiving end of someone else's grace. There were several moments throughout my life when someone stepped in to help me. I've been blessed to have people serve my needs when I wasn't in a position to do so for myself. Now that I'm on the other end of my struggle, it's so important to pay it forward by serving others.

As you prioritize your own healing, begin to think about who you can serve and what causes are important to you. I've found that purpose is rooted in service. When you begin to serve, you can discover purpose and as you operate in purpose, you will find that your purpose is much greater than your pain.

What organizations in your community serve a group or a cause that you are passionate about?

_____

_____

_____

_____

_____

_____

_____

_____

_____

_____

_____

_____

_____

_____

_____

Think about what or who you needed when you were struggling in your life, now how can you be who/what you needed for someone else?

_____

_____

_____

_____

_____

_____

_____

_____

_____

_____

_____

_____

_____

_____

Chapter 7

Amazing Grace

Gratitude is the gateway to abundance. When you focus more on what you have, it has the power to minimize the pain and frustration of what you lack. When you give more power to what is going well, it reduces the sting of what is going wrong. You see, what you focus on is what expands. Practicing gratitude daily really altered my mental state. Whenever I found myself giving too much attention to my problems, or whenever frustration was fueling my day, I would immediately start to think of all the things that I was grateful for. I would stop myself right in the middle of negative thinking, and I would begin to express thanksgiving for every single thing I could think of that I really appreciated. This was extremely effective because it's difficult to be angry and grateful at the same time.

I want you to make a habit of starting your day with gratitude. Make a list of all of the many things in your life that you are grateful for. It can be something as minimal as waking up on time, not having to stop for gas because the tank is already filled, to being thankful for life, health and strength in your body. Every day when you wake up, I challenge you to find one good thing to focus on and express sincere gratitude toward.

Create your Gratitude list

_____

_____

_____

_____

_____

_____

_____

_____

_____

_____

_____

_____

_____

_____

_____

No matter how traumatic your life has been, know that there is still room for goodness, but you have to invite it in and embrace it. You have to abandon toxic responses that repel good things in your life. The better you become, the more you will attract the desires of your heart. Your life was not meant to be a revolving door of negative experiences. Even in the midst of dysfunction, there will always be a beacon of hope. There will always be at least one thing that is working for you. Your job is to seek it out, honor it and be grateful for it.

Chapter 8

Free to be

An uncaged bird has no limits, and neither do you. No matter what version of your story you find yourself living right now, know that you have the power to create an alternative ending. What will the rest of your story read? What does an emancipated version of you look like?

After you release the weight of worrying about what anyone else thinks about you, and once you come into the realization of who you really are, you are free to evolve.

I challenge you to expand the vision that you hold for who you are, what you're capable of and the potential that you possess. Growing up, I was always drawn to bright colors and abstract art. I would draw and doodle throughout my notebooks. This was therapeutic for me because it allowed me to escape whatever I was feeling at the moment. I could be dying on the inside, but doodling provided an outlet to express my emotions. If I was feeling trapped, a fine stroke of my pencil liberated me. There is a sense of peace in finding a healthy way to release what's bottled up inside of you. Have you ever noticed that some of the most prolific artists and creatives tend to have the most colorful stories. Many have suffered with depression, anxiety, homelessness, abuse and addiction. When you're fighting a war within, what you create gives you an opportunity to make something beautiful despite emotional burdens.

The mere fact that you can still create a masterpiece in the middle of your suffering is an indicator of just how much power you have. It shows that we can still function under pressure, and that our ability to create is much more powerful than the fleeting emotions that we feel.

When we get too caught up in how we feel, it's so easy to forget what we know. I need you to know that you deserve happiness, wholeness and good health. When I decided that I wanted to experience happiness, I had to work on my emotional injuries. When I decided that I wanted to be whole, I had to be intentional about filling myself up with things that empowered me. I started to get very clear about what I needed in order to be at my best. Implementing and maintaining a consistent workout routine has been critical. Taking care of my body is my way of taking action in my healing. You can't have faith to heal and then skip out on the work. Eating healthier, engaging in healthy relationships with those who inspire me, working with a therapist, assessing my weaknesses, highlighting my strengths, forgiving others and offering myself more grace have all been keys that have played a significant role in helping me to adopt the courage to establish a brand new me.

Having the courage to begin again, to learn and unlearn, to forgive, forget, release and grow has not only changed my life, but has changed my outlook as well. I am free to be who God has called me to be, I am free to live and love without limits, I am free to be imperfect knowing that even with my flaws I am still a beautiful masterpiece. I am free to experience inner peace, I am free to walk away from things that are not good for me, I am free to start over, to learn from my mistakes and to make a huge impact in the lives of others. I refuse to be burdened by my past, I refuse to live within the restraints of pain. I am free to operate in purpose and to establish personal power. I am free to be me. I am free to live courageously authentically.

I didn't always know my worth, I didn't always believe in myself, I didn't always make the right choice. I haven't always been focused on my personal growth and I haven't always been fearless, but I made the choice to adopt courage, to abandon my fears and to embrace life outside of my comfort zone. I made a choice to evolve beyond merely surviving in order to thrive. This is my story, my truth and my process. I am currently growing into the best version of myself, my hope is that reading this book has encouraged you to do the same.

Daily Reminders to Live a Happy & Courageous Life

1. Always remember that better days are coming

2. Forget the mistake, remember the lesson

3. Choose to keep fighting even though times are rough

4. Don't give up on yourself

5. Decide to let go of the past so that you can create the future that you want

6. Remind yourself daily that you have a beautiful soul that radiates in a vibrant and beautiful form.

7. Affirm that all is well in your mind, body and soul.

8. Honor yourself by honoring your boundaries

9. Have the courage to keep moving forward

10. You have everything you need on the inside of you

11. Be bold enough to stand up for what you believe in

Personal affirmations are a very powerful tool to help you make positive declarations in your life.

Here are some of my favorite.

<u>Affirmations</u>

I wake up with a peaceful mind and a grateful heart

I am capable of overcoming hard things

I am deserving of love, kindness, forgiveness and redemption.

I am happy, healed and whole

I am worthy of greatness, in fact I was designed for it

I am a candidate for massive breakthrough

I am not a victim I am a victor....

Now add your own empowering message to the list

_____

_____

_____

_____

_____

_____

_____

_____

_____

_____

_____

_____

Survival Kit

Survival tools to keep in your tool box

Ways to nurture yourself.

- Listen to your favorite music

- Pray

- Call someone who you trust

- Take a bubble bath

- Dance

- Sing

- Read a book that you enjoy

- Take a walk

- Exercise

- Watch the sunrise

- Watch the sunset

- Journal

Resources

The National Domestic Violence Hotline:
> 1800-799-SAFE (7233)/ 1800-787-3224 (TTY)
> https://www.thehotline.org

The National Sexual Assault Hotline
> 1800-656-HOPE (4673)
> https://www.rainn.org

Suicide Hotline
> 1800-273-TALK (8255)

Sidran Institute Traumatic Stress Education & Adovcacy
> (410) 825-8888
> https://www.sidran.org

National Center for Victims of Crime (NCVC)
> (202) 467-8700
> www.ncvc.org

National Center for Posttraumatic Stress Disorder (NCPTSD)
> (802) 296-5132
> http://www.ptsd.va.gov

National Child Traumatic Stress Network
https://www.nctsn.org

Center for Relationship Abuse Awareness Education & Action
http://stoprelationshipabuse.org

EMDR International Association (EMDRIA)
www.emdria.org

The Courage Creed

I am enough

I am good enough,

I am beautiful enough,

I am strong enough,

I am powerful enough

I am who I am

I am who God says I am

and that's enough

I give myself permission to grow

I am bold enough to try again

I have enough courage to face my fears

I lack nothing

My purpose is greater than my pain

I will not settle in a dark place

I will allow my light to shine through

I will no longer tolerate anything

toxic in my life

If it doesn't help me grow then

it has to go

I have enough power to push through

I have enough courage to let go

I have enough greatness

to make an impact

I am enough

Enough is enough

Deep Breathing

Deep Breathing: a relaxation technique performed by purposefully taking slow, deep breaths. When practiced regularly, deep breathing provides both immediate and long-term relief from stress and anxiety.

How Deep Breathing Works

During periods of anxiety, the body triggers a set of symptoms called the stress response. Breathing becomes shallow and rapid, heart rate increases, and muscles become tense. In opposition to the stress response is the relaxation response. Breathing becomes deeper and slower, and the symptoms of anxiety fade away. Deep breathing triggers this response.

Instructions

Sit back or lie down in a comfortable position. Close your eyes, if you would like to do so. When you're learning, try placing a hand on your stomach. If you breathe deeply enough, you should notice it rising and falling with each inhalation and exhalation.

> **Inhale.** Breathe in slowly through your nose for 4 seconds.

> **Pause.** Hold the air in your lungs for 4 seconds.

> **Exhale.** Breathe out slowly through your mouth for 6 seconds.

Tip: Pucker your lips, as if you are blowing through a straw, to slow your exhalation.

> **Repeat.** Practice for at least 2 minutes, but preferably 5 to 10 minutes.

<u>Tips</u>

- If it isn't working, *slow down*! The most common mistake is breathing too fast. Time each step in your head, counting slowly as you do so.

- Counting out your breaths serves a second purpose. It takes your mind off the source of your anxiety. Whenever you catch your mind wandering, simply return your focus to counting.

- The times we use for each step are suggestions, and can be lengthened or decreased. Lengthen the time if it feels natural to do so, or decrease the time if you feel discomfort.

What are Personal Boundaries?

Personal boundaries are the limits and rules we set for ourselves within relationships. A person with healthy boundaries can say "no" to others when they want to, but they are also comfortable opening themselves up to intimacy and close relationships.

A person who always keeps others at a distance (whether emotionally, physically, or otherwise) is said to have *rigid boundaries*. Alternatively, someone who tends to get too involved with others has *porous boundaries*.

Common traits of rigid, porous, and healthy boundaries.

Rigid Boundaries	Porous Boundaries	Healthy Boundaries
Avoids intimacy and close relationships.	Overshares personal information.	Values own opinions.
Unlikely to ask for help.	Difficulty saying "no" to the requests of others.	Doesn't compromise values for others.
Has few close relationships.		Shares personal information in an appropriate way (does not over or under share).
Very protective of personal information.	Overinvolved with others' problems.	
May seem detached, even with romantic partners.	Dependent on the opinions of others.	Knows personal wants and needs, and can communicate them.
Keeps others at a distance to avoid the possibility of rejection.	Accepting of abuse or disrespect.	Accepting when others say "no" to them.
	Fears rejection if they do not comply with others.	

Most people have a mix of different boundary types.

For example, someone could have healthy boundaries

at work, porous boundaries in romantic relationships, and a mix of all three types with their family.

The appropriateness of boundaries depends heavily on setting. What's appropriate to say when you're out with friends might not be appropriate when you're at work.

Some cultures have very different expectations when it comes to boundaries. For example, in some cultures it's considered wildly inappropriate to express emotions publicly. In other cultures, emotional expression is encouraged.

Types of Boundaries

Physical boundaries refer to personal space and physical touch. Healthy physical boundaries include an awareness of what's appropriate, and what's not, in various settings and types of relationships (hug, shake hands, or kiss?). Physical boundaries may be violated if someone touches you when you don't want them to, or when they invade your personal space (for example, rummaging through your bedroom).

Emotional boundaries refer to a person's feelings. Healthy emotional boundaries include limitations on when to share, and when not to share personal information. For example, gradually sharing personal information during the development of a relationship, as opposed to revealing everything to everyone. Emotional boundaries are violated when someone criticizes, belittles, or invalidates another person's feelings.

Material boundaries refer to money and possessions. Healthy material boundaries involve setting limits on what you will share, and with whom. For example, it may be appropriate to lend a car to a family member, but probably not to someone you met this morning. Material boundaries are violated when someone steals or damages another person's possessions, or when they pressure them to give or lend them their possessions.

Intellectual boundaries refer to thoughts and ideas. Healthy intellectual boundaries include respect for others' ideas, and an awareness of appropriate discussion (should we talk about the weather, or politics?). Intellectual boundaries are violated when someone dismisses or belittles another person's thoughts or ideas.

Sexual boundaries refer to the emotional, intellectual, and physical aspects of sexuality. Healthy sexual boundaries involve mutual understanding and respect of limitations and desires between sexual partners. Sexual boundaries can be violated with unwanted sexual touch, pressure to engage in sexual acts, leering, or sexual comments.

Time boundaries refer to how a person uses their time. To have healthy time boundaries, a person must set aside enough time for each facet of their life such as work, relationships, and hobbies. Time boundaries are violated when another person demands too much of another's time.

Brief checklist
of trauma symptoms

Check the symptoms below that you experience. Include symptoms you have even if you are not sure they are related to a traumatic event.

I experienced or witnessed a traumatic event during which I felt extreme fear, helplessness, or horror.

The event happened on (day/month/year) _____.

What happened? _____

1.

I have symptoms of re-experiencing or reliving the traumatic event:

☐ Have bad dreams or nightmares about the event or something similar to it. Behave or feel as if the event were happening all over again (this is known as having flashbacks)

☐ Have a lot of strong or intense feelings when I am reminded of the event

☐ Have a lot of physical sensations when I am reminded of the event (for example, my heart races or pounds, I sweat, find it hard to breathe, feel faint, feel like I'm going to lose control)

2.

I have symptoms of avoiding reminders of the traumatic event:

☐ Avoid thoughts, feelings, or talking about things that remind me of the event

☐ Avoid people, places, or activities that remind me of the event

☐ Have trouble remembering some important part of the event

3.

I have noticed these symptoms since the event happened:

☐ Have lost interest in, or just don't do, things that used to be important to me

☐ Feel detached from people; find it hard to trust people

☐ Feel emotionally "numb" or find it hard to have loving feelings even toward those who are emotionally close to me

☐ Have a hard time falling or staying asleep

☐ Am irritable and have problems with my anger

☐ Have a hard time focusing or concentrating

☐ Think I may not live very long and feel there's no point in planning for the future

☐ Am jumpy and get startled or surprised easily

☐ Am always "on guard"

4.

I experience these medical or emotional problems:

☐ Stomach problems

☐ Intestinal (bowel) problems

☐ Gynecological (female) problems

☐ Weight gain or loss

☐ Pain, for example, in your back, neck, or pelvic area

Meet Katherine Wald

Katherine Wald is a licensed psychotherapist, certified EMDR therapist, and ADHD coach in private practice in Miami. She earned her bachelor's degree magna cum laude from Georgetown University and her master's degree with honors from the University of Pennsylvania.

Katherine is a certified clinical supervisor and has been in practice for over 15 years. She is trained in multiple modalities, including: cognitive behavioral therapy (CBT), dialectical behavioral therapy (DBT), eye movement desensitization and reprocessing (EMDR), psychodrama based experiential work, art and play therapy, mindfulness based stress reduction, meditation, and emotional freedom technique (EFT).

In addition to her work in private practice, Katherine co-founded the nonprofit organization, Inspire Transformation (IT). Through her work with IT, Katherine provided therapy to gender-based violence survivors and trained women in rural South Africa and Namibia on how to counsel survivors in their communities.

As a therapist who specializes in trauma and dissociative disorders, Katherine bears witness to the power of healing on a daily basis. She feels strongly that "you are not what happened to you" and that your past does not need to define your present. She feels honored to be able to contribute to this important book.

For more information, please visit:
www.katherinewald.com